SELECTED POEMS

SELECTED POEMS

Ai Qing

TRANSLATED BY *Robert Dorsett*

FOREWORD BY *Ai Weiwei*

CROWN
NEW YORK

Published in the United States by Crown,
an imprint of Random House, a division of
Penguin Random House LLC, New York.

CROWN and the Crown colophon are registered
trademarks of Penguin Random House LLC.

Library of Congress Cataloging-in-Publication Data
Names: Ai, Qing, 1910–1996, author. | Dorsett, Robert Hammond, translator.
Title: Selected poems / Ai Qing; translated by Robert Dorsett; foreword by
Ai Weiwei.
Description: First edition. | New York: Crown, [2021]
Identifiers: LCCN 2021029864 (print) | LCCN 2021029865 (ebook) |
ISBN 9780593240724 (hardcover) | ISBN 9780593240731 (ebook)
Subjects: LCSH: Ai, Qing, 1910–1996—Translations into English. | Chinese
poetry—20th century—Translations into English. | LCGFT: Free verse.
Classification: LCC PL2833.I2 S45 2021 (print) | LCC PL2833.I2 (ebook) |
DDC 895.11/51—dc23
LC record available at https://lccn.loc.gov/2021029864
LC ebook record available at https://lccn.loc.gov/2021029865

Printed in Canada on acid-free paper

crownpublishing.com

9 8 7 6 5 4 3 2 1

FIRST EDITION

Translation by Robert Dorsett

Book design by Barbara M. Bachman

CONTENTS

FOREWORD

IN THE TWENTY-ONE years between my birth in 1957 and 1978, my father, the most prominent Chinese poet in modern history, was deprived of the right to write by his government. Writing poetry was the most precious part of his life, and when he was young, Ai Qing said, "If one day my life leaves poetry, it would soon end as well." Unfortunately, it did not end there. He left poetry but did not end his life; the regime only deprived him of his writing, forcing him to withdraw from the reading public. For many years, he was forbidden to touch pen and paper, and was sent to the Gobi Desert in the remote province of Xinjiang, where he cleaned the communal toilets of a labor camp and underwent ideological reforms day after day.

When I was growing up, my father was not engaged in writing. He tenaciously faced all kinds of misfortunes brought by fate. He was known to be tolerant, upright, and selfless. Misfortunes never shook his trust in justice, and he never lost his outspoken innocence; he remained optimistic and open-minded.

In his work, Ai Qing tells the story of an ancient nation in the East over the past hundred years as it bid farewell to the heavy burden of feudalism and imperialism. This land was recovering from the violent revolution of the twentieth century to become a new country. In the process, a generation of people experienced an arduous struggle, only to exchange the past repression for a new totalitarian rule as China became the country with the harshest control over freedom of thought and speech in human history. Today its political system erases history and culture and has destroyed the language formed over generations, abusively transforming it into crude political propaganda, a cliché of mediocrity, leaving aesthetics and morals in ruins.

In contrast to this, Ai Qing's poems are characterized by his sincerity, a powerful tool for resisting autocracy and oppression. As an anti-feudal, anti-imperialist intellectual, fighting for national liberation, individuality, and freedom of speech, he left a rich legacy of the people's struggle.

I never expected to write the preface for my father's poetry collection and present it to an audience of readers that he never dreamed of. During the Cultural Revolution, a few decades ago, he and I burned his entire collection of books and manuscripts together.

The differences between my father and me cannot be erased by the biological bond. I was born into a different world than he was. However, I found a great affinity with him, which gradually emerged after more than half a century: we are both sealed by the same fate to fight against tyranny, and to endlessly reflect upon and discuss the concept of freedom. My understanding of him is deeply rooted in the interpretation of liberation of the individual and the crises faced by humanity.

As a kind of faith, Ai Qing's writing brought both joy and sorrow to his life. He sacrificed for his beliefs in order to survive under the harsh political environment. His use of vernacular Chinese and his love for simple truths make his expression a powerful reality; his inner truth makes his poetic thinking flow like a stream of spring water, even in the driest season. In the most suffocating years, Ai Qing never betrayed his beliefs; it was he who showed me the courage needed when aesthetics and morals are marginalized. Against the aesthetic mediocrity of despotism, poetry is the key to wisdom, and the mortal enemy of banal politics. The existence of poetry is proof that the soul cannot be conquered, that no matter when and where, poetry comes the closest to reflecting inner truth, and the creation of another accepted truth is subversive to the desert of power: independent and unruly, as an unyielding existence, poetry is salvation.

AI WEIWEI

FEBRUARY 4, 2021

TRANSLATOR'S
INTRODUCTION

ALTHOUGH AI QING (1910–1996) is one of the most important poets in Chinese history, little is known of his work by English-language readers. Hopefully, this volume—written for anyone who loves poetry and is interested in Chinese literature—may go some small way toward a remedy.

Ai Qing wrote during one of those times in Chinese history when flux and turmoil laid a fertile ground for poetry. The fall of the imperial Manchurian rule and the establishment of the People's Republic, the conflict between Nationalist and Communist forces, the new imperialism of the invading Japanese armies, and the struggle among warlords, all combined with a loss of faith in traditional values and institutions to foster an upsurge in intellectual and political movements. No longer could literature be isolated from the common people. Adapting the expansive free-verse forms of Whitman and Mayakovski, Ai Qing addressed his readers directly; his work was made all the more powerful by the fact that everyday readers could understand it.

Ai Qing was born the son of a rich landowner. Fearing a

fortune-teller's warning that Ai Qing would bring bad luck, his father sent him as an infant to be raised by a poor tenant family. As a young man, Ai Qing left China to study abroad. In Paris, he studied the work of Renoir and Gauguin as well as that of Kant and Hegel. On his return, he joined the League of Left-Wing Writers and was arrested by the Nationalist government. The first poem to bring him fame was "Dayanhe"; tenderly exploring his relationship with the wet nurse who raised him, it was written in a prison cell. In 1957, he was arrested again during the Anti-Rightist Campaign, and was sentenced, along with his wife and children, to a work camp. During this time, he was not allowed to lift his pen, leaving a large gap within his oeuvre. After the fall of the Gang of Four, he was permitted to resume publishing.

In translating Ai Qing's poems into English, I felt I had an opportunity to delve deeply into the work of a poet and to do so freely, without prior judgment. My purpose was to create translations that combined Ai Qing's principles of passion, concision, sincerity, and clarity of rhythm. And I wanted them to stand as poems on their own.

There are many good English translations of Ai Qing in print, as well as many finely written critical works. I encourage readers to look them up. With some trepidation, I offer the addition of my own translations to this legacy. But I should make clear: since all decisions were made by me from the original Chinese texts, any mistakes or confusions are my sole responsibility.

Ai Qing often uses natural symbols—the sun and fire—to signify the advent of the newer, happier age he hoped for and believed in, but he also wrote poems of protest, when politics failed his ideals. Throughout all his work, there is a deep and personal passion, a genuine love for human beings, and pity for the oppressed, a pity that, combined with profound lyricism, reaches deep into the heart of the reader.

ROBERT DORSETT

SELECTED POEMS

DISTANT SUNLIGHT

sunlight on distant desert sand

a boat glides along a river darkened by clouds

dark wind

dark clay and gravel

darkness

of the traveler's mind

—sunlight plays

and sparkles on distant desert sand

FEBRUARY 1932
ON THE SUEZ CANAL

TRANSPARENT NIGHT

I.

Transparent night
. . . peals of laughter erupt from the fields . . .
a gang of drinkers sights
the drowsy village, trudges
into it—laughing,
shouting . . .

In the village,
a dog bark
shakes, in the immensity
of the firmament,
the disjointed stars.

In the village,
the gang hurries
through sleepy streets,
through a sleepy marketplace,
into a bright tavern.

Wine, lamplight, drunken faces,
dissolute laughter in a crowd

Let's go,
let's go to the slaughterhouse,
let's drink beef broth . . .

2.

A gang of drinkers walks to the outskirts,
walks into a gaping, lamplit door
—and into the blood stink, heaps of flesh,
the cowhides' raw, rancid stench,
and the bellowing men, the bellowing men . . .

Kerosene lamplight, like prairie fire,
inflames the dozen clay-colored faces
of those who on the grasslands
eke out a living.

This is our place for good times,
these the faces we know;
we pick up steaming beef bones,
open our mouths, gnaw and gnaw . . .

wine, wine, wine,
give us wine

Kerosene lamplight, like prairie fire,
reflects upon the blood,
the butcher's gore-stained arms and hands,
the gouts spattered on his forehead.

Kerosene lamplight, like prairie fire,
plays upon our flame-like muscles

—within—
the tinder of anger, bitterness, hatred, spite . . .
Kerosene lamplight, like prairie fire,
lays bare—in every corner—
the sleepless:
drunks
vagrants
robbers
cattle thieves

wine, wine, wine,
give us wine

3 .

While stars shine,
shivering,
we go . . .

Peals of laughter erupt in the fields . . .
a gang of drunkards leaves
the sleeping village, enters
the drowsy grasslands,
laughing, shouting . . .

Night! Transparent
Night!

SEPTEMBER 1932

DAYANHE—MY WET NURSE

Dayanhe—my wet nurse;
her name comes from the village where she was born,
she was a child bride;
Dayanhe—my wet nurse.

I am the landlord's son . . .
Drinking Dayanhe's breast milk, I grew to be her son;
Dayanhe, in nurturing me, nurtured her family,
and I, I was nurtured by drinking your milk;
Dayanhe—my wet nurse.

Dayanhe, today I see the snow and think of you:
your weed-strewn grave oppressed by snow,
the eave tiles weathered on your old, boarded home,
your few square paces of mortgaged land,
the stone bench before your door long since mantled
    with moss.
Dayanhe, today I see the snow and think of you.

With your large, generous hands you cradled, caressed me:
after you built the cooking fire,
after you brushed ashes from your apron,
after you tasted whether the rice was done,
after you placed the dark bowl of bean paste on the
    pitch-black table,
after you patched your sons' clothes ripped by thorns on the
    mountainside,
after you bandaged your small boy's hand cut on the
    firewood ax,

after you picked lice one by one from your husband's and
     sons' undergarments,
after you fetched the first egg of the day's laying,
with your large, generous hands you cradled, caressed me.

I am the landlord's son . . .
After I finished nursing milk from Dayanhe's breasts,
I was taken back to my birth parents' home.
Ah, Dayanhe, why do you cry?

I became a guest in my birth parents' home,
I ran my fingers over the furniture's embossed,
     red lacquered flowers,
I stroked the gold embroidery on the duvet on my parents'
     bed,
I looked blankly at the wooden tablet above the lintel
     inscribed with the motto I couldn't understand: "Family
     Love and Happiness,"
I stroked the silk of my new clothes sewed with seashell
     buttons,
I looked at the little sister I didn't know in my mother's
     arms,
I sat on a varnished bench warmed by coals in an
     earthenware basin placed beneath,
I ate refined rice, milled three times.
Yet I was discomforted; I was ashamed. I became
a strange guest in my birth parents' home.

Dayanhe, in order to live
after her milk ran dry:

used the two arms that once embraced me for labor:
with a smile, she washed our clothes,
with a smile, she carried baskets of vegetables, rinsed them in
    the freezing pond at the village outskirts,
with a smile, she sliced turnips that were frozen solid,
with a smile, she scooped in her bare hands rotted wheat for
    hog feed,
with a smile, she stoked the fire beneath the meat stew,
with a smile, she carried a winnowing basket to the city
    square filled with sun-dried soybeans and wheat grain;
Dayanhe, in order to live
after her milk ran dry,
used the two arms that once embraced me for labor.

Dayanhe dearly loved the child she nursed;
for him, she busily minced winter rice to make New Year's
    candy;
and for him, who quietly stole to her home outside the
    village,
for him, who ran to her side and called out "Ma,"
Dayanhe pasted the garish picture he painted of the God of
    War on the wall alongside her stove,
Dayanhe praised highly to her neighbors the child she
    nursed.
Dayanhe once had a dream she could tell no one:
She dreamt she attended her nursling child's wedding
    reception;
she sat in a resplendent, brightly decorated hall;
a beautiful bride tenderly addressed her as "Mother."
Dayanhe dearly loved the child she nursed.

Dayanhe died before she woke from her dream;
When she died, the child she nursed was not by her side;
When she died, the husband, who repeatedly cursed her,
    shed tears,
And each of her five sons wept bitterly;
When she died, she called out softly her nursling
    child's name;
Dayanhe died;
When she died, the child she nursed was not by her side.

Dayanhe went with tears in her eyes,
with more than forty years of life's insults and humiliation,
with the bitterness shared by countless serfs and slaves,
with a coffin costing four coins, laid out with a few bunches
    of straw,
with a few square feet of earth in which to bury her,
with a handful of ashes from burnt paper money;
Dayanhe went with tears in her eyes.

This is what Dayanhe doesn't know:
Her drunkard husband died;
her eldest son turned to banditry;
her second son died in the smoke of gunfire;
her third, fourth and fifth sons
pass their days bullied by bosses and landlords;
and I, I write to curse this unjust world;
after I drifted about for a long time and returned home,
on the mountainside, on the wild steppes,
and I meet my brothers, we're more intimate than six or
    seven years ago;

This, this is because of you, Dayanhe, quietly sleeping,
this is what you do not know.

Dayanhe, today the child you nursed is in prison;
I offer this elegy written for you,
for your noble spirit beneath the common earth,
for the arms you stretched out to embrace me,
for your lips that kissed me,
for your tender yet earthy complexion,
for the breasts that nourished your child,
for your sons, my brothers,
for, everywhere upon this earth,
all the nurses like my Dayanhe and their children,
and for loving me as she loved her own sons, Dayanhe.

Dayanhe, nursing your milk I grew to be your son;
I honor you;
Love you.

JANUARY 1933

VISIT TO AN OLD RESIDENCE

Hush. Listen:
from a corner between walls
the slow, pensive notes
of an antique flute
carved from animal horn . . .
You are in
medieval Paris
—remote from the tumult,
cloistered in the "sacred book" of Paris.
When I, following the shifting tide
of the times,
during my volatile youth,
journeyed by foot,
from a far distant lodging,
and arrived where you reside—
I was like a road-weary traveler
in a foreign land
entering a church
amidst unrelenting, harsh city noises,
to gain a bit of cherished peace.
I climb the dark staircase;
quietly, you guide me
into a large, dimly lit room
imbued with the fragrance of old wood.
With sentiment
I gaze at furniture
in the style of the Louises,
fine bone porcelains from Persia,
and, in a carved, mahogany bookcase,

the complete volumes
of Racine, Molière and Hugo.
As a breeze
softly ruffles the
white window curtains,
you begin to sigh,
and, with your warm, deep breaths,
the large wave-shaped flounce
on your delicate silk blouse
gently heaves;
with humor in your blue eyes,
stilled in pensive thought,
you're curious about what fancy
I harbor in my heart.
Before me,
your long, golden hair
unfurls, and I imagine
a sea of many waves
permeating to the pale, purple horizon.
With composure, you sway
your supple, full body
—and it makes me think faintly
of the days of Raphael
replete with such loveliness . . .
my eyes,
slow, tardy in the low light, I listen
to the modulations
of your refined voice
as you relate:
stories of spirits and men,

stories of sunlight
and of Eros,
stories from the poems of de Musset
in which tears
turn into pearls . . .
Let me sit,
and, without saying a word, face you,
and, inside an old, forgotten dream,
make a long meandering journey,
holy, immaculate in its love;
but, listen!
That antique wooden wall clock
betrays its schoolmaster's dignity;
comically,
it affects the shrill tones of a singing rooster;
now, what welcomed me, and I quietly came,
urges me, and I quietly go.

1 9 3 3 — 1 9 3 5

THE CRY

At its piercing sound
the sun's eye opens, releases torch-like flames;
at its piercing sound
the wind spreads warm, tender arms;
at its piercing sound,
cities awaken . . .

This is spring;
this is spring's morning:

from a place of darkness
I look longingly toward
a universe of glittering clarity,
where,
life is turning, moving,
where,
time is a briskly spinning wheel,
where,
radiance swiftly flies . . .

from a place of darkness
I look pensively, longingly,
toward a universe
where clarity, light, leap like waves;

this, the sea of the cry of life!

MARCH 1933

MY SEASON

Today I can no longer sit
on a bench, watching
droves of pigeons
trek circles about park statues.
Only the rain patters
like footsteps of a passerby;
now and again I hear in the calmness
the gusting rain's long, drawn-out, monotonous paces,
and a real, inescapable melancholy
grips my young man's heart.
Along the endless walkways,
small droplets, fraying from
the branch tips of path-side trees,
scatter on my bare neck;
I reach out, grasp
the park's iron railing,
and it's like touching the fingers
of a bored housewife weary of loving and hating,
and I feel, with a fresh, pleasant chill,
this is my season . . .
let me whistle the unending syllable of a note
rising, broken and fluttering,
into the emptiness,
toward all those paths no one treads . . .
Whenever I think of early spring's
vainglory, the overbearing blaze of summer's
heat, and cruel winter's
heartless passage, I want, day after

day, year after year, to hold on to
these somber autumn colors
steeped with such endless melancholy.
Dark hatred, radiant love,
have nothing to do with me:
and life's anxieties,
all burning hope for fortune,
have fallen with the rustling
of these first withered leaves
that tell me everything I have faith in lies here.
Ah, Autumn!
I ask you, with your same ash-gray raindrops,
come with me—I'm weary listening
to this petty, tedious talk,
these pretenses of righteousness—
and, guarded, with my precious bond of silence,
stride with me across the city square
splashed with dirty water from passing cars,
wandering toward places
for which I know no name.

1933–1935

THE LAMP

Hope that looked toward the horizon
now lies in this oil lamp—
For the sky's farther than hope can reach!
Arrows of light obliterate the distance
into blank nothingness;
then what makes my trembling fingers
gently stroke the brilliant forehead
of this oil lamp?

1933–1935
IN PRISON

THE SUN

From ancient gravesites,
from generations in darkness,
from the brink of trenches
of the human dead,

startling slumbering mountains,
wheeling flame over sand dunes—
the sun plunges toward me . . .

His encompassing brilliance
breathes life into rivers and trees,
makes crowded branches sway,

makes the waters surge toward him fiercely,
joyously, in song . . .

He appears—and I hear
—wakened like long-hibernating
larvae from beneath winter soil—
the people
congregating in open squares
talking loudly,

as cities far around beckon him
with electric light and
gleaming steel—

Then his flaming hand rips away
my pettiness, rends open my narrow mind,

and discards my depleted soul
upon a riverbank—

And I have faith in the regeneration of
human beings—

SPRING 1937

A CONVERSATION WITH COAL

Where do you dwell?

I dwell in years deep within mountains;
I dwell in years within craggy stone.

What is your age?

My age is greater than the mountains,
greater than the stony crags.

From what times have you kept silent?

From the times dinosaurs ruled the forests,
from the times the earth's crust first shook.

Did you die, buried beneath indignation?

Die? Oh, no, no, I'm still alive—

Please, touch me; touch me with flame!

SPRING 1937

SPRING—

Spring—
peach trees flower in Longhua—
flower from those nights
those nights spattered with blood
those nights without stars
those nights scraped by winds
where you hear the widows' choking cries
where this ancient earth
always a parched, ravenous beast
laps the blood of young men
the blood of sons of the stubborn men
where, through long winter days
through the season of ice and snows
through boundless, bone-wearying expectation
when those bloodstains, those trails of blood
from myth-like nights
from those deep, pitch-black eastern nights
burst from numberless buds
decorating everywhere south of the Yangtze with spring.

People ask: Where did spring come from?
I say: From outside the city, from graves.

APRIL 1937

LIFE

Sometimes
I flatten my bare arm
against a wall;
the chalk-white plaster
brings out the ruddy glow
of healthy flesh

green waters channel the earth
blue veins course through my arms

my five fingers
are five red branches;
within them circulates
the blood of the man who
plows the earth.

I know
this is life:
let it be burdened
by love's suffering and the hardships of survival,
let it struggle for breath,
strain beneath the age's bitter yoke,
let it prance, agonize, laugh, cry
—spur itself onward
till, spent, it slumps down.

This is
what should be
and what I will

in these days of expectation—
I use the pale, dead ash
of my misfortune to bring out the vivid red
of a fresh, new life.

APRIL 1937

THE RESURRECTED LAND

Days of rot and decay
sink into the river—
Let rushing waters scour them—
quickly scrape them clean of stain.

And upon banks—everywhere
spring steps—
lush flowers, thick grasses, flourish—
from dense woodlands,
hundreds of birds, faithful to the season,
broadcast irrepressible songs—

Oh, you sowers of seed,
now is the time to sow—from your willing,
hard labor, the great earth will bear
golden beads of grain—

Now is the time;
you—Oh, you mourning poets—
to wipe away the suffering of the past,
let hope wake in your long, too long
aggrieved hearts,

because our once dead earth,
beneath this clear and unclosed sky,
comes alive.

—Hardship will be memory—
In the earth's warm breast
our fighters' spilled blood
flows afresh—

JULY 1937

SNOW FALLS ON CHINA'S LAND

Snow falls on China's land;
cold blockades China . . .

Wind,
like a grief-stricken old crone,
dogging closely,
reaches out an icy claw,
tugs at the coat neck of the passerby,
jabbering in a tongue ancient as the land,
incessantly clamoring, entreating . . .

From the woodlands emerge
fleeing horse carts—
You, China's farmers,
in fur caps
braving the blizzard,
where are you heading?

I tell you:
I too am the offspring of farmers,
from the lines
grief carved deeply into your faces;
I know well
the people of the steppes,
their arduous years.

And I
am no happier than you
—several times adversity's great waves,

couched in time's rushing waters, have risen
and engulfed me, swept me away—
Wandering or imprisoned,
I've lost the most valuable days
of my youth;
my life
is like your life
—and, like yours, broken.

Snow falls on China's land;
cold blockades China . . .

Down the river
on this snowy night,
the light from a small oil lamp slowly drifts;
the lamplight glows
from within a rotting, dark canopied boat:
Sitting there, head hanging,
who are you?

—Ah, you,
disheveled-haired, dirty-faced young woman,
is it that
your home
—your happy, warm and blessed home—
has been, by the cruel, despotic enemy,
burnt down?
Is it that,
in a night like this,
stripped of your men's protection,

with deathly terror, you
suffered the teasing play of the enemy's bayonet?

Coughing, in a freezing night like tonight,
our numberless
aging mothers
huddle in houses not their own,
like foreigners,
not knowing onto what journey
tomorrow's vehicles take them
—And
China's roads
are rough and rugged,
muddy and mired.

Snow falls on China's land;
cold blockades China . . .

Passing the steppes in this snowy night,
passing regions of darkness gnawed through
by war's beacon fires,
numberless, the land's harvesters,
who've lost their breeding livestock,
who've lost their fertile fields,
packed into life's filthy alleyways of despondency,
in a world of starvation,
to face dark, overcast days,
to reach out two trembling arms,
begging.

Like this snowy night,
China's disasters, its miseries,
are vast and pervasive.

Snow falls on China's land;
cold blockades China . . .

China,
I write on a night, without the glimmer of light,
this powerless poem.
Can it give you warmth?

DECEMBER 1937

DURING THE JAPANESE INVASION

THE NORTH

One day
a poet from the Keerqin Prairie
said to me
"the North is pitiable"

That's right
the North is pitiable;
from beyond the frontiers, desert winds
swept
the North bare of everything living and green,
chafed the days clean of radiance
—a flat, dull and ashy yellow light
sheathes an irremovable layer of sandy mist;
from the horizon the rush of howling winds,
bringing fear,
crazily
scrapes the earth;
the untamed plains
freeze in cold December winds;
villages, hillsides, riverbanks,
crumbled walls and abandoned graves
all shrouded with a clay-colored melancholy . . .
a solitary passerby,
body bent forward in the wind,
shielding his face with his hands,
breathing laboriously,
step after step
struggles forward . . .
A few donkeys

—those dumb animals with doleful eyes
and sad, droopy ears—
bearing
the heavy burden of the land's suffering,
slowly tread
the North's
narrow and sparsely traveled roads . . .

The small rivulets have shriveled,
their beds crisscrossed with ruts of wagon wheels;
the land of the North, and its people,
eagerly thirst for
the refreshing waters of life-giving springs!
The withered forests,
and stunted, low-roofed huts,
sparse and gloomy,
spread out beneath the sky's murky tent;
in the sky
no sun can be seen;
only vast formations of wild geese,
fearful flocks
striking their black wings,
crying out unease and sorrow,
flee from these desolate boundaries,
flee
to the green foliage of the South . . .

The North is pitiable;
the surging, turbid billows
of the ten-thousand-li Yellow River
deluge the far-reaching North

with torrents of disaster and misfortune;
generations of wind and ice
have cut into
its landscape
a terrain of hunger and deprivation.

And I,
a traveler from the South,
still love this grief-stricken Northern country.
The sandy wind that lashes my face,
the glacial, bone-piercing air,
that never makes me curse;
I love this pitiable land,
revere
this stretch of unending wilderness
—I see
our ancestors
leading flocks of sheep,
playing reed pipes,
steeped in the great desert's yellow twilight;
we tread
this layer of ancient, soft and crumbling loam
where our ancestors' bones lie buried
—this, the land they opened to cultivation,
for thousands of years
they were here
struggling with nature that dealt them hard blows;
they protected the land
without suffering a bit of indignity,
they died
bequeathing the land to us—

I love this pitiable country,
this wide-open, barren earth
that brought with it our plainspoken language
and our generous manner;
I believe this language and generosity
so firmly rooted in the life of this land
can never be destroyed;
I love this pitiable country,
this ancient country
—this land
that nurtured everything I esteem:
the world's oldest,
most resolute people.

FEBRUARY 1938

BEGGARS

In the North
beggars loiter along both banks of the Yellow River
both sides of the railroad tracks

In the North
beggars use their most badgering voice
to cry out suffering
tell you they come from disaster areas
from war-torn zones

Hunger is terrifying
it robs the old of their humanity
teaches the young to hate

In the North
beggars affect an unrelenting stare
and fix their eyes upon you
watch whatever food you eat
the way you use your fingernails to pick your teeth

In the North
beggars doggedly hold out hands
dirty black hands
they never draw back
and demand the dole of a copper coin
from anyone
even soldiers who haven't one coin.

SPRING 1938

DUSK

The forest at dusk is dark and gentle,
a clear light glitters
on marsh and pond
and I am beguiled by caresses
of a breeze that brings,
again and again, fragrance
of the fields . . .

I've always loved the breath of farmlands,
no matter where I wander,
when I walk through fields at dusk,
I feel a sense of loss
and I'm restless remembering
the aroma of manure from domestic animals
along old country roads
and, in the livestock pens
outside the village,
the dry grass scents.

JULY 1938
WUCHANG

WANDERING ON AN AUTUMN DAY

I love watching
on a bright, crisp autumn day
cloud shadows crisscross the steppes,
and, scattered like stars
throughout the deep-lying hollows,
white-haired goats
crop and chew the sprouting grass, with no one
to care for them;
a newly laid dirt road, bordering a small brook,
bends into dappled woodland
and emerges farther in the distance
upon a sun-drenched mountain slope . . .
we are not going to visit long-parted friends,
but because, on this unfamiliar path,
the shadows play with sunlight,
so we stroll leisurely, feeling
a simple, carefree exhilaration . . .
Clouds mass together in the empty sky,
surge and scramble;
raindrops drift down mixed with sunlight,
then the rain falls harder and harder,
still, the steppes stretch out in four directions
bathed in the sun's glow.
Near a mountain village
we sit on the roots of several large trees
sheltering against the rain.
The rain, like a hastily deployed regiment,
swerves northward . . .
and, in an instant, the air's moist and cool . . .

we step upon the slate stone roadway
glistening-wet with rainwater,
pass over a newly built stone bridge,
pass along a mountain ridge,
and into the deep wildwood
that, with its endlessly spreading shade,
receives us—
elm, camphor, pine,
and many trees we can't name
cluster in that wildwood . . .
when we stride in
and sit on the grass,
innumerable white egrets startle—
beating wings,
with parted beaks hooting piteously,
they arise from dense green thickets—
doubtless, hermits long cloistered here.

AUGUST 1938

I LOVE THIS LAND

If I were a bird,
I'd use my harsh voice to sing:
of this land raked by tempest blasts,
of these perpetually agitated torrents of indignation,
of these winds ceaselessly fanning the flames of outrage,
and of that inimitable warm and tender dawn
breaking from the forest midst
—after I die,
even feathers and fine down rot into dirt.

Then why do my eyes tear?
Deep run the currents of love . . .

NOVEMBER 1938

WINTER FOREST

I love to walk through the forest in winter—
the forest without sunlight
the forest raked by dry, parched winds
the forest threatened by snow

lovely, the days without tinge of color
lovely, the days without bickering birds
fortunate, the man who walks alone through the
  winter forest—
I'll pass stealthily, stalking like a hunter
unwilling to kill his prey . . .

FEBRUARY 1939

AUTUMN

With the season mist arrives—
steadily, rain tarries
over reaped fields . . .
Here, plowed-up black mud
and green sprouts
from grain left over in furrows
weave a vast, dark, and undulating surface,
lingered over by that late autumn visitor,
the unfaltering rain . . .
people lie low
behind their houses' thick-black walls;
only two horses, with splashed brown manes,
slowly plod toward the horizon
seeking out the wild plains' last green . . .

AUTUMN 1939

AUTUMN MORNING

Cool, refreshing, this morning,
the sun's just risen, this morning,
the village, sorrowful this morning.

A little bird, white feathers circling its eyes,
perches on the black roof tiles
of a low, squat hut;
as if lost in thought, it gazes at
the many-hued clouds bannering the sky.

It's autumn;
I've been in the South a year;
this place hasn't got the tropics' vitality;
no coconut palms surge to the skies;
already my pent-up heart is sad

but today, as I'm about to go,
I feel uneasy
—China villages:
everywhere the same filth, gloom, poverty,
but not one I'd want to leave.

SEPTEMBER 1939

WATER BUFFALO

Ash-gray hide,
dry, tough, a dull matte,
crook'd horns,
hard, solid as ice;
your entire carcass
damp, congealed with ditch muck;
large, gloom-brimmed eyes
gaze into vast and desolate fields—
Without utterance,
you strain against the curved, bitter
and painful yoke,
and, beyond endurance, your muzzle
chugging white mist,
plod with laboring, exhausting steps,
break up frozen ground.

WINTER 1939

WILD LANDS I

A light drizzly haze shrouds the desolate plains . . .

Shrouded, the distance . . .
And I can't see the pine forests that yesterday
stood against a bright, cloudless sky;
I can't see the plaster-white cliffs
that, behind those pines, once blazed in sun.
In the foreground, barely discernible,
a murky-yellow dirt road twists;
on both roadsides spread
the parched, raven-black fields . . .

Those long-forsaken fields—
jumbled clods of upturned earth;
wild grasses, dry, withered,
entangle
rotting stalks of grain;
dirty, red-ocher flats,
tinged with the orange of scorched tea leaves,
permeate the broad, sweeping ash-gray haze . . .
—only a few
scattered clumps of green turnips
break through white hoarfrost
to ornament
the banal, dull crudity
of these shabby fields.

Water, stagnant in contiguous bogs,
due to endless drought,

quickly dries;
a few
pale-brown levees stagger
haphazardly through the opaque glare;
water reeds and lotus leaves,
lush, blue-green in former days,
have long since settled
into silt,
leaving several
gnarled, withered tree trunks and branches
standing blankly
in the lazily rising
marsh vapor.

Before me, a mountainside sprawls;
a road curves up the slope
following the land's
undulations,
then turns downward
and disappears into a sparse copse of trees . . .
on both sides of the ash-yellow road
gloom and apprehension
emanate from rambling grave mounds
and the black-stone tablet
about to be buried in the smoky air.

—The same static chill
pervades everything, lays desolation bare . . .

Slag-yellow and winding road!
People trek, and trek,
in different directions,
forever led by the same shadow,
locked in the same fate;
with endless labor and starvation before them
they await disaster, illness, death—
people with no way out of the wild lands—
who could be happy?

And yet
I'm intimate
with these wintry fields—
upon the bone-piercingly cold winter ice,
I walk upon uneven embankments,
along edges of these forsaken marshes,
and over the gloomy, dark-brown mountainside,
my footsteps grow heavy, painful
—like an aged ox, having plowed the fields,
hauling back its weariness . . .

And the fog—
a turbid, pale-gray ash,
vague and unfathomable,
spreads before me—
utility wires
fade pole by pole
opening the limitless, vast expanse . . .

Woeful and unrestrained,
toilsome and impoverished wild land . . .

Not a sound
—everything's asphyxiated by fog,
only
from shadowy clumps of bushes
the racket
of grim, awe-struck sparrows
shivering feathers,
chittering . . .

The few bunched huts
bordered by bramble and reed–woven fences,
the same firewood
piled haphazardly against walls,
the same tattered clothing dangling atop bamboo poles,
cry
the people's meaningless, unending toil;
the listlessly rising kitchen smoke from
frost-coated tree bark roofs,
mixing with fog,
draws a picture
of ineluctable poverty . . .

The people in these hovels
pass gloomy, insipid days . . .
caged in life's shadows . . .
As if daylight's never there,
they breathe the same air as the livestock,
their beds like animal stalls;
their coarse, hard bedding's
like piles of clay
dull gray and hardened . . .

The freezing cold, starvation,
ignorance and superstition
seize these small hovels
with an iron grip . . .

From the fog, a farmer emerges,
shouldering a bamboo basket
that holds a few scrawny bunches of scallion and garlic;
his cloth hat tattered beyond repair,
his face filthy as his clothes,
his hand, deeply cracked by cold,
thrust inside his waistband,
his bare feet
treading the ice-caked road;
he doesn't make a sound
except for the low squeaking of his shoulder pole;
bit by bit
he vanishes, engulfed by the fog before him . . .

Oh, wild lands—
can you endure sorrow, injustice,
forever, and still be silent?

A light drizzly haze shrouds the desolate fields . . .

JANUARY 1940

WINTER MARSHES

Winter marshes,

desolate, as an old man's heart,
strewn with the years' bitter struggles, his heart;

Winter marshes,

dry, as an old man's eyes,
the radiance ground by toil into ashes, his eyes;

Winter marshes,

sparse as an old man's hair,
the grasses scattered with ash-white frost, his hair;

Winter marshes,

lonely, as a mournful old man
hunched beneath night's dropping curtain, an old man.

JANUARY 1940

TREES

One tree. Another tree.

Stand distant, alone.

Wind, air,
inform their isolation.

But under cover of mud and dirt
their roots reach
into depths unrevealed,

entwine unseen.

SPRING 1940

MOUNTAIN ELM

Spring thunderstorm
roughly shakes the mountain elm
Spring thunderstorm
violently jolts my heart

Proud, erect and haughty,
brown leaves blow in mountain wilds,
tinged with earth's love, melancholy,
roots clutch rock and mud,

happiness, solemnity,
a friend of sunlight and mist,
borrows words from the wind, occasionally,
unscrolls anguish in the wilds

suffers stinging cold, flailing rain,
sighs, awaits the thunderclap,
and the cruel ax:
chock, chock.

SPRING 1940

THE GAMBLERS

Against the dingy feet of city walls,
on corners of soot-black tenements,
numberless gamblers squat in circles,
tensely gaping at each dice toss.

Filthy, broke, muddled, yet fervid,
they rock, jam heads together, then
winners' shouts, losers' curses, accompany
the clattering of tossed copper coins.

Women hold babies, stand aside;
disheveled, they stare. The babies,
hungry, struggle and cry. But the women are
transfixed by their men's shifting luck.

Men squat and stand; stand and squat,
slap thighs, shout, giddily surprised;
their faces redden; tight mouths drop—
They're trying to turn poverty around.

They lose and win, win and lose, but
the filth, rags, the folly, won't change.
Nightfall: they scatter back, disgruntled,
into soot-black tenement rooms.

1940

CROWDS

Electricity whines in cables—cracks across
an arc, like ten, twenty piano keys struck at once
—and often, from within me, deafening voices
break out, reverberate through space.

One drop of water amazes me; I stare—
suddenly, the vast, tumultuous Yangtze emerges;
I open my mouth—and gasp—as if through that
small opening ten thousand people breathe.

When I touch my bounding pulse—I feel,
in my heart's shudder, the tempestuous tides of blood;
their sufferings, desires, with mine, intermingled—
When did their blood pour into my veins?

What's over there? So many, so many,
numberless feet, hands, heads packed together,
in windows, on streets, at ferries, bus stands.
What are they doing? Thinking? What do they want?

The enormity's frightening: the second
I think of it I'm not myself—but a number,
a number that bit by bit enlarges so immensely
it boggles me; I'm staggered, stunned.

When I rest, countless feet tread on my heart.
When I walk, my heart's a noisy intersection—
I sit here—people crowd the streets—and suddenly,
I see myself among them, churning in dust . . .

1940

WILD LANDS II

Maize ripened fiery, like these days,
alongside fields of newly cut hemp;
beneath the scorching sun,
a straw-hatted farmer bends,
reaches, picks from
green soybean plants, the tender leaves.

Beneath the still, vacant sky,
untold kinds of chirping insects,
in lowly yet intricate chorus,
praise the natural world;
the cicadas' insistent din,
and the wood doves' hankering cries,
pour from dense, variegated wood thickets
at the slanting mountain base.

Yesterday, at dusk, I heard water rush
through the narrow gorge,
now, it's stopped;
as I walk from the turf of the dark woodland,
there's only the urgent, staccato knocking
of a woodpecker drilling hollow wood.

The sun radiates through tree gaps,
the sun radiates from heights we cannot grasp,
the sun casts searing heat that makes
the bent-bodied farmers grateful they don't need
to lift their heads,

the sun sets all living things afire,
the sun bestows fervor into all living things.

Ah, my back's soaked with sweat;
I walk past long, long rows
of legumes and melons
that grip bamboo trellises with thin,
whisker-like tendrils
(shame and pride contend in my heart),
once more I come to the mountainside,
stop, wipe sweat from my brow, and rest
beneath a mountain elm.

Simple yet lackluster,
tall, broad, yet scorned,
my friend, the mountain elm,
every day I call to visit,
and often, beneath its shade,
for many long hours, wordless,
I gaze over the wilderness;

The wilderness—so vast, so savage . . .
so familiar
yet so fearsome,
a rolling, surging land,
a brutish sea
of rock and trees . . .

Untamable, spiked peaks

like blue-green sea breakers,
doggedly rise and fall;
the black boulders,
inextricably jumbled;
the countless roads,
seemingly unconnected,
yet tangled, knotted together;
and those village huts,
those lowly, pitiable huts,
every one isolated, scattered
like stars;
Their windows,
at first glance indifferent,
glare at each other with disdain,
and those mountain peaks
gripped with malice
stand bitterly, mutually opposed;
the wild woods, far and near,
like thick, bristling hair,
messily tangled,
fearsome, silent,
store in their deep, unfathomable shadows
the grievance of a thousand years.

And below,
in those deep, sunken valleys,
hectare after hectare of contiguous land,
people besieged,
encircled by rocks,
live out their fated years
from childhood to death in old age;

without rest, they strain their bodies
to plow the unyielding land,
day after day dripping sweat,
panting beneath the heavy yoke
of poverty and hard labor . . .

Rebelling against fate,
I left my decrepit village.
Today, I return.
Why should I hide—
I am this wild land's son.
Look at me: alone I walk across the mountains,
with slow, painstaking but staggering steps,
like an exhausted water buffalo;
through my body, dark, gloomy, like pine bark,
flows stubborn, anguished blood;
Often, like the moon,
I quietly gaze
upon the vast and rugged wild land.
Or, like a tramp,
walk humbly
in the dusky haze
over perilous mountain passes;
in my heart, my vaguely aching heart,
continuously surge
my life's irrepressible yearnings!
And every day
I am plagued
by sorrows,
I lie on the mountainside,
shaded by the mountain elm,

and, looking over the expanse of wild lands,
for a long time, without a word,
let my heated thoughts and passions
dissolve into the distance
of its undulating crags, its sunlight
and shadows . . .

1 9 4 0

NIGHT 1

Again, the night is clear.
When I get up, stand by the window,
I feel I'm floating
upon a vast yet tranquil sea.

Mountains, lush forests, without number,
countless acres of grain-rich valleys,
lie bare in the moonlight—
beautiful, no matter what the time.

I know there's suffering there.
They live with beasts of burden—
They crawl, gasp for breath, sigh.
Their eyes fixed upon the sodden earth.

Now, they should be quiet,
like drunks sprawled upon filthy mattresses.
Their day's trickling, dirty sweat
traded for night's pitch-black sleep.

The moon isn't bright for them.
Each night the stars pass over their roofs.
Sadly, I listen to them toss and turn, hear
their exhausted, unsettled snores.

NIGHT 2

Why do you drink again?
Why do you set brains, lungs, afire?
All night you toss, turn, with bad dreams.
Awake: pallid moonlight floods the window . . .

When, behind dark clouds, moonlight hides,
dogs bark more piteously,
more desolate, more forsaken
—Could people be lost again
in the depths of these terrifying mountains?
And what bandits
crouch in tight crevices?
Or perhaps pass along
the ridges?

JULY 1940

MY FATHER

PART I

Lately, I've had dreams of my father—
His face revealed a tenderness I hadn't known before
that showed he had forgiven me.
His speech was gentle,
as if all his purpose, and all his effort,
were only to protect his son.

Last spring, he wrote several times,
imploring, in conciliatory terms, that I return;
he wanted to impart to me several important matters,
matters to do with land and property,
but I didn't heed his wishes
and didn't make a move to return home.
I feared family entails responsibilities, responsibilities
that would destroy a young man's life.

One day, in May, when the pomegranates bloomed,
harboring disappointment, he left this world.

PART 2

I, his first son,
was born during the final year of the Manchu reign,
when he was a student in middle school.
He was already twenty-one years of age.
He maintained a queue, wore a long,

traditional gown, and appeared
kindhearted, even tolerant. His corpulence;
ruddy brown complexion; large,
round and protuberant eyes; his ears
pasted closely behind his cheeks; made everyone
proclaim his physiognomy lucky, so he reckoned
he could be content and self-preserving.

Pleased also with a favorable horoscope,
he passed insipid, ordinary days,
sprawled on a bamboo couch,
puffing a water pipe, sipping yellow rice wine,
reading *Strange Tales from a Chinese Studio*,
prattling about female spirits and magical foxes.

When my father was sixteen, his father died.
My grandmother, a child bride raised by the family,
was bullied constantly by her husband's concubines.
My father's elder brother, an opium addict,
gave gambling parties, and toyed with women.
But he, my father, by cultivating a life
of self-discipline and strict moral principles,
became a good son to his mother
and a good husband to his wife.

He accepted Liang Qichao's thought,
and, realizing "world progress has no limits,"
became a disciple of reform.
He was the first, in this poor, isolated village,
to cut off his raven-black queue.

A reader of the magazine *Far East*—
a subscriber to the Shanghai newspaper *Shenbao*—
a member of the Multinational Savings Cooperative—
the clock, displayed in the front of his hall, struck the hours;
the kerosene lamp in his room burned.

The town store, inherited from great-grandfather,
sold local and foreign goods, foodstuffs,
wine—anything one could want.
It provided cloth enough to dress the family.
We could get anything—daily articles, snacks for tea,
simply by presenting a small folded paper.
For 360 days, thirty-nine employees toiled, and,
at year's end, the master took all the profits.

He owned several acres in the village;
scores of tenant farmers hovered about him.
The four farmhands our family hired every year,
together with a maidservant and an elderly housekeeper,
cocooned him in comfort.

No passion! Avoid risk!
For his own benefit and self-interest,
he strove to establish "a modern family,"
and sent his daughters to missionary school,
constrained his sons to learn English.

For discipline: he slapped and whipped,
and became, within his family, a tyrant.

Thrift was the dogma he gave us,
obedience the creed he gave us.
He demanded painstaking study,
forced close attention to grades.
He realized knowledge is an important commodity—
First, it's a decoration to be worn;
second, it preserves wealth.
The honored guests in his home were:
a retired major general,
a middle school teacher of Chinese in the provincial capital,
economics and law students from the university,
the town bailiff
and the county-seat magistrate.

He perused world atlases,
studied meteorology and astronomy.
From the theory of evolution he learned
monkeys are our human ancestors.
When he performed sacrificial rites,
he assumed a look of meek sincerity.
But in his heart he was very clear—
Regarding tenants come to pay their levy,
adopting the graven image of the God of Hell
proved more expedient than Darwin's theory.

Feckless, he expected "progress."
Clueless, he welcomed "revolution."
He knew it was "the tide of the times."
But quailed before the coming storm
and stood at a distance, waiting.

1926
The Nationalist Revolutionary Army
set out from the south, passed through our village.
At that time, I wanted to take the entrance examination
for the Whampoa Military Academy
but he remained silent,
his eyes clouded over, and he gave no answer.

The storm of revolution came and went.

Countless brave, young heroes
were sacrificed to the age.
Sickened by the horror, the agony,
my mind, like a boat ripped of sails,
drifted on foggy and turbulent seas . . .

Landlords, wanting their sons rich and holding office,
pressured them to study economics and law,
but I dabbed a brush into paint,
scrawled a landscape
and a laboring farmer.

A young man's imagination and ardor
spurred me to leave home.
So I could travel far into distant cities,
I thought up countless ruses and stratagems
to gull my father into sympathy.

One evening, he lifted a floorboard
and took out one thousand Mexican silver dollars.

His face dark, his hands shaking,
he counted as he cajoled:
"After a few years, come home.
On no account let good times keep you away."

When it was time to leave,
he accompanied me to the edge of the village,
I didn't dare consider
the weight of hopes he placed upon me,
and in my heart, I prodded myself,
"Ah, leave, quick—
leave these pitiable fields,
leave this low, miserable village,
go wander alone,
wander in freedom."

PART 3

A few years later, a dejected shadow
returned to that run-down village.
Empty-handed, bereft
—but for a few seditious books,
a portfolio of impassioned paintings—
and deeply ingrained with a
colonized people's shame and enmity.

July, I was locked in jail;
August, I was sentenced.
Because of his dashed expectations,
my father cried until dawn.

In those dark times
he tirelessly wrote complaisant letters,
beseeching me to be a "model" for my brothers and sisters,
to bring myself in line with "the family's wishes."
Using clichéd language, playing
upon my emotions, he arranged for me my well-being
in order to take my mind prisoner.

When I regained freedom,
he anxiously wanted my return—
He mailed me
barely enough fare to get home.

He repeated what others said
(Heaven knows where he heard it!):
China does not have a capitalist class;
no American-style big business;
no cold-blooded exploitation, no extortion.
He said, "Never have I
oppressed an employee.
If they really have a revolution,
what'll happen to me?"
Then he spread his account books,
opened a thick ledger of grain royalties,
and, as his fingers ran over the abacus,
he looked at me with kind eyes,
smiled through his long beard,
and entreated me, with supplicatory words,
to heed my siblings' future.

Finally, he became enraged—
He scowled, bit his lower lip,
and looked fury-stricken at heart.
Drumming the table angrily with his fingers,
he resented his son's indifference,
who treated his home
as an inn for travelers,
who looked down on his inheritance
with contempt.

In order to retrieve myself from this wasteland,
in order to search after the highest ideals,
I again left my village.
Even if my feet were swollen and bleeding,
I'd never stop going forward . . .

My father died;
he contracted bloating of the abdomen, and died.
From then on he couldn't restrict me;
What more do I have to say?

He was a common man—
fainthearted, content with his lot.
In these turbulent times,
he passed his life peaceably.
Like countless landlords in China,
complacent, conservative, frugal, self-serving,
he made this poor, out-of-the-way village
his enduring empire;
the inheritance he received from his ancestors
would be the inheritance he left his sons,

never to be diminished or increased.
So it was—
For this, I pity him.

Today, my father
lies peacefully beneath the soil.
When he was carried to his grave,
I didn't raise a pennon to show his soul
the way across the river of death
into another life, nor did I don coarse hemp clothes
to mourn him—

Hoarse-voiced from shouting, I threw myself
into the fire and smoke of the war for liberation.

My mother wrote, bidding me to return,
to put family matters into final order;
but I did not want to be buried myself,
so, cruelly, I ignored her wishes.
Grateful to the war for giving me inspiration,
I set off in the opposite direction from the village—
because—by everything I know—
the world has no higher ideal
than to give allegiance—not to family—
but to the millions of people—
that is my sacred belief.

AUGUST 1941

THE TIMES

I stand beneath low house eaves,
rapt in the sight of wild mountain mists
and the wide, spacious sky;
for a long, long time I've felt something uncanny
—I see a blaze that, like the sun,
rouses me;
from the far distance, a steady, grave rumble,
bears the howling shriek of wind and rain,
and comes, roaring, tumbling . . .

I'm enthralled, cry joyously;
when from that snow-clad, cloud-shuttered mountain
I hear the grinding, jolting of huge wheels over rugged
    ground,
my heart seeks it, beating fiercely,
like a bridegroom hastening to his wedding
—even though I know it could never give me
a festival's wild exhilaration
or the raucous laughter of shows in public squares,
and it's even more cruel than the scene of a massacre,
still I hasten to it
with all the passion that I can unleash from a life.

I'm not a weakling, not self-satisfied;
I don't pity or deceive myself;
I'm not glutted with what this world has given me,
whether it's honor, whether disgrace,
or whether people look at me with disdain or blind hatred,
or with eyes sparkling in delight,

but when they don't understand, I feel empty;
I ask for more, yes, more,
give me a living world;
I keep my two arms extended;
I ask to scale high mountains;
I ask to reach across vast seas;
I welcome louder acclaim, noisier condemnation,
the most irresolute grudges
and the most fatal blows—
it makes me want to lift myself from the ditch of these
    dark times . . .

No one's anguish can be greater than mine;
I am loyal to the times, pledge myself to the times,
and yet I am silent,
unwillingly silent, like a condemned prisoner
before he's taken to the execution grounds;
I'm silent because my words are not loud
like the early summer thunderclaps rolling through dark,
    clouded skies,
and I cannot give voice to the eagerness, cries,
that I would devote to this rapture, this joy;
I love these times more than anything I've loved before;
for its arrival I'd gladly give my life,
give my body and soul;
I'd lower myself before it;
I'd lie down and let it, with its hoof-like feet,
trample me into dust.

DECEMBER 1941

THE SUN'S WORDS

Open your windows;
open your wooden doors;
let me in, let me in,
into your little rooms.

I bear bouquets, gold and yellow;
I bear the forest's fragrance;
I bear warmth and radiance;
I bear the mantling dew.

Quickly rise; quickly rise;
lift your heads from your pillows;
open your lash-covered eyes,
so you see me enter.

Open your windows; let me
scatter flowers, fragrance, warmth,
light and dew, to freshen the air in your
hearts' long-shuttered rooms.

JANUARY 1942

WILDFIRE

Set these black nights ablaze—
From high mountain peaks
reach out your fiery hand,
stroke the night's broad chest,
stroke its ice-cold,
deep-blue chest—and from the
highest tips of tossing flame
send sparks floating down,
like swarming immortals,
into the incalculably dark
and freezing hollows—illuminate
the dim and hazy dreams
of sleeping souls, so they, for once,
join your ecstatic dance—

Set these black nights ablaze—
Higher! Ever higher!
Let spirited forms
leap from earth into the high airs,
and, with your affecting lights,
rouse our weary world!
Urging with fiery glow,
raise a cry!
Make all those night-clad eyes
gaze upon you.
Make those night-gripped minds
shudder at your call—

O laughing flames . . .
O trembling flames . . .

Listen, from what far, deep recesses,
like a cataract—surges praise.

1 9 4 2

THE REEF

A wave, and a wave
strike, and again strike

the foot of the stone,
explode, scatter spray.

Its face and its bulk
hacked by many blades.

Yet the reef stands,
smiles, regards the sea . . .

JULY 1954

THIS CLEAR, RADIANT MORNING . . .

This clear, radiant morning:
the plane glides high into air;
white, flowering clouds smile;
my heart's ablaze like the sea.

I wrote poems about suffering,
and, as I wrote, I grieved;
my hardship's at long last over;
now, I'll sing this new day.

JULY 1954

OVER THE PACIFIC OCEAN

PEARLS

In emerald seawater
you absorb the essence of sun,
embody a rainbow's prism,
nacreous as morning clouds;

contemplating
the shape of dew upon petals,
delighting
in the purity of crystal:
these thoughts, nurtured in your heart,
solidify, pearl after pearl.

JULY 1954

MOUNTAIN SPRING

Mountain song
famous far and near;
your voice is clearer
than spring water.

The mountain's high,
the water's deep;
drink, and one's singing
is mellow, sweet.

Ordinary people
do not come here.
To climb such a mountain,
who perseveres?

Only two kinds of
birds alight, linger here:
daytime, the lark;
evening, the nightingale.

AUGUST 1956

MORNING SNOWFALL

Snow falls, endlessly falls,
snow falls, soundlessly falls,
pure snow blankets the courtyard,
pure snow blankets the roofs,
the whole world's quiet,
the whole world's at peace.

I watch the drifting snowflakes
and I remember long, long ago,
I remember a summer forest,
dawn-lit that forest,
the sun just risen,
everywhere dew glistens,
a small, barefooted child
walks into the morning light,
his face fresh as a flower,
he sings a soft, low whispering song,
he holds a bamboo pole in one hand,
he lifts his delicate head,
his bright shimmering eyes
search for the cicada
calling through luxuriant foliage,
in his other hand he totes
a string of green objects
—ants, a golden beetle, dragonflies,
tied together
to a long blade of foxtail grass,
all this
I remember.

It's been a long time since we were in the forest,
there, fallen leaves have spread all over
and no one's shadow falls.
But I've never forgotten the child
and his soft, low murmured song;
right now I don't know which hut he's in,
watching snowflakes drift endlessly,
perhaps he wants to throw snowballs in the forest,
perhaps he wants to skate upon the pond,
he could never know
someone's thinking of him,
on this morning, in this falling snow.

NOVEMBER 1956

FISH FOSSIL

lively your gestures,
vigorous your spirit,
as spindrift on sea waves
rises and falls;

by mischance a volcano erupts,
perhaps an earthquake,
you lose your freedom
and enter dust;

a million years pass,
a geology team
uncovers you from a rock,
vivid as when alive;

but you're silent,
without even a breath,
fins and scales preserved exactly,
unable to budge an inch;

in absolute paralysis,
you can't react,
can't see sky or water,
can't hear breaking waves;

gazing at a fossil
even a simpleton learns
without movement
there's no life:

to live is to struggle,
to struggle is to evolve,
give it all you can
before Death arrives.

1 9 7 8

THE MIRROR

Only a flat surface
yet unfathomable,

it loves the truth,
wouldn't hide a flaw.

Honest, if you search within it;
you always find yourself:

red-faced from liquor,
hair freckled with snow.

Some delight in it,
because they're beautiful.

Others look away,
because it is too frank.

There are even those
who'd love to shatter it.

1 9 7 8

GREETING AN INTOXICATING SPRING

1.

I couldn't tell what it was; did you hear?
these past nights, erupting from the river,
again, and again, a kind of cracking—
Ah, it's river ice thawing;
freed, the water flows quickly:
Chunk upon chunk of ice bump together,
jam into packs,
like a crowd, as far as can be seen, jostling,
laughing, entering a theater.

The long-awaited spring has come—
The time of sowing, cultivating, is here.
The time of abundance is here.
Who doesn't love spring—
Even if, after the snow and ice melt,
the roads thicken with muck,
even if we plod through vast bogs,
we go to welcome her, because she brings
expectation and warmth.

2.

We've had springs of lies;
we've had springs of banishment;

we've had springs of imprisonment,
we've had springs of sorrow . . .

We've crawled like snails
along foundations beneath walls.
We've worn away time,
like disciples of a lama, beating
small, skull-shaped wooden drums,
chanting sutras.
Meanwhile,
military vehicles, in countless thousands,
from the entire outside world,
fly along our high-speed expressways,
and MiG-25 fighter jets, at any time,
can strike like lightning across
our sacred blue skies.
What faces us is an incomparably
difficult trial.

After turbulence and unease,
we've at last come to our senses.
We've smashed through layer upon layer
of solid ice, released time's surge.

3 .

Finally, we live without fear;
finally, we pass our days with pride;

finally, we're armed with
a powerful, unflinching confidence;
and, like the Kazakh people,
in their festival, *chasing the maiden*,
we jubilantly welcome spring.

She comes, really comes.
You can smell her fragrance,
feel her body's warmth—
Together, small birds sing in trees;
fawns leap in the forest . . .

Sound our sirens:
greet the new era's dawn.
Fire a twenty-one-gun salute:
greet the season's advent.

All our musicians play,
all our poets compose,
and interweave words, music, into a masterwork
to greet this intoxicating spring.

1979

BONSAI TREES

Like artifacts from antique times—
these trees transmogrified into metal:
trunks into bronze; branches, iron wires;
leaves, verdigris with greenish copper patinas.
In decorous, formal courtyards, suffering
no winter's cold, summer's heat, they're
displayed on lacquered, sandalwood stands
to enhance their prodigal stature.

In truth, they're relics of affliction;
their original character's long gone.
In flowerpots of many shapes, sizes,
they suffer injury, bitter constraint;
at every growth stage, they're twisted
with iron wires, razed by knives.
Manipulated—with no freedom to expand—
as one part grows, another's stunted;
with imbalance as the goal, they're
fragments, designs never complete.
Like bent-backed, rachitic old men
flaunting freakish deformities, some
thrust out trunks like bellies, some expose
legs of knobby root tubers, leaving a few
contorted branches and leaflets no larger
than sesame seeds to prove they're young.
Like wounded, war-sickened soldiers,
they live out debilitated lives.

But plants and flowers
need their own province,
where root fibers absorb soil's nutrients,
leafy branches take in rain and sun,
with freedom to flourish, thrive healthily;
happy on this common earth, harmonious, they
receive Mother Nature's tender care, pour forth
their individual sweet perfumes.

Now they're turned inside out:
young, they're old, and old, young,
to please someone's curiosity,
glorify some greenskeeper's ingenuity.
Soft, pliable, easily twisted,
mute vegetation, they bow beneath the blade.
You can say it's a kind of art:
a parody that writes
the end to freedom.

FEBRUARY 1979

SEA AND TEARS

The sea's salty,
tears are salty

too. Does the
sea become

tears? Do tears
become the

sea? A billion
years of tears

converge into the
sea. A day will come

when sea and
tears are sweet.

1979

THE PRICKLY PEAR

You love the fragrant tulip;
I love the prickly pear.

It thrives in hot climates;
the desert's its hometown.

Unbending in sandstorms,
It's unbelievably stubborn.

Fearless in the fiercest drought,
it blossoms just the same.

But raise it on a windowsill,
it dreams of the open sea.

1 9 7 9

THE WALL

A wall, like a knife,
cuts the city:
here, the east,
there, the west.

How high is the wall?
How thick?
How long?
Higher, thicker, longer,
it can't compare to China's Great Wall.
Higher, thicker, longer,
it's still a vestige of history,
the wound of a people.
No one wants a wall like this.

Three meters high is nothing,
fifty centimeters thick is nothing,
forty-five kilometers long is nothing,
a thousand-fold higher,
a thousand-fold thicker,
a thousand-fold longer,
how could it stop
the red-lit clouds,
the rain, wind, sun across the sky?

How could it stop
the wings of migrating birds,
the nightingale's song?

How could it stop
the flow of water or the air?

And how can it stop
a billion people
whose thoughts are freer than wind?
whose resolve is more deeply rooted than earth?
whose aspiration is more infinite than time?

MAY 1979

LOST YEARS

It's not like losing cloth-wrapped bundles;
they can be reclaimed in lost and found.
It's not even possible
to know where they've gone—
some dissipate in bits and pieces,
some are lost over ten, twenty years,
some in bustling cities,
some in remote wastelands,
some in a bus station amidst the swelling crowd,
some beneath solitary oil lamps.
Lost years aren't pieces of paper
that can be picked up—
but water splashed upon the ground:
the sun dries it; no shadow can be found.
Time is a flowing liquid—
no sieve, no net, retrieves it.
Time can't be solidified;
No matter if it becomes a fossil, even after
thousands of years it can be recaptured from stone.
Time is vapor: smoke chugging
from the locomotive of a racing train!
Lost years are like a friend; after
ties are broken and grievances pass,
you suddenly get the news: Your friend
has long since left this world.

AUGUST 1979

TIGER COWRY

Beautiful tiger stripes,
body glittering with flame,
what polished your radiance?
what burnished your glow?

More delicate than fine porcelain,
harder than a pure jewel,
like goose eggs: smooth, elliptical,
no blemish bigger than a pin tip.

How many years in despair's sea,
tossed about by vast breakers,
a body, all jadestone armor,
protecting a life too easily hurt.

If a chance wave hadn't thrown me ashore,
I'd never hope to see such fine sunlight.

DECEMBER 1979

THE RUINS AT JIAOHE

As if a caravan's passing through—
amidst the crowd's clamor
the clang of camel bells.
As of old, there's a bustling market—
carriages rushing like water,
horses like dragons—

But no—the luxurious palace
has fallen into devastation and ruin,
and of a thousand years of joys and sorrows,
of meetings and parting,
nothing can be found.

Those who are alive, live on fully—
don't hope earth keeps a trace behind.

1980

DREAM OF THE MAN WHO
CULTIVATED FLOWERS

IN HIS COURTYARD, a man who cultivated flowers planted several hundred bushes of China Rose. He reckoned in this way he could see flowers bloom every month of the year. There are many varieties of China Rose, and his friends from all around, who knew he had this fondness, devised ways to have others bring these roses to him as gifts. When the roses bloomed, the flowers varied in color but not in kind, which gave the courtyard a busy uniformity. Every day, in order to better nourish these flowers, he painstakingly irrigated, mulched, fertilized and pruned the branches and leaves.

One evening, the man had a startling dream: Just as he was cutting the withered branches from a rosebush, a crowd of flowers thronged into the courtyard—it was as if all the flowers of the world had come. Each flower looked at him with knitted brow and tears of dew on its eyelashes. Amazed, he stood up and looked around at each one in turn.

The first to speak was the Peony: "I have my pride; I certainly wouldn't care to be your courtyard's uninvited guest, but today, at my sisters' request, I accompanied them."

The Water Lily followed: "When I awoke on the bed of my pond by the forest edge, I heard the clamor of my sisters as they passed through the forest, so I followed along."

The Morning Glory bent her delicate body and parted her lips. "Could it be possible we're not beautiful enough?"

The Pomegranate, incensed, said, flush-faced, "Your indifference hides disdain."

The White Orchid said, "You must have insight to comprehend the beauty within our character."

The Prickly Pear added, "Those who only love gentle people are themselves weak. We're endowed with an indomitable, unswayable spirit."

Now the Winter Jasmine, who heralds spring, said, "I bring faith."

And the Orchid, "I value friendship."

The flowers, having spoken the words that fit them best, finally said together, "To be understood is a blessing." And now the China Roses said, "The truth is we are lonely; if we could be together with our sisters, we would be much happier."

The multitude of flowers said, "Those who are favored are truly fortunate. We have been neglected for a long time. Behind the backs of the favored ones lurk many with grievances." After they had finished, the flowers suddenly disappeared.

When he awoke, he felt heaviness in his heart. He paced up and down the courtyard and thought, "It's the flowers' nature to have self-resolve. To blossom is the flowers' right. Because of favoritism, I have engendered discontent in all the flowers. More and more I believe my world has become too narrow. Without comparison, ideas become muddled: Only if we have the short can we measure the long, only if we discern the small can we gauge the large, and only if we have the homely can we realize the beautiful . . . From this day on, my courtyard will become a country for all flowers. Let our lives grow wiser; let all flowers in their own season bloom."

JULY 1956

EXCERPTS FROM
THE NOTEBOOKS

(SELECTED BY *Ai Dan*)

Poetry, more than any other literary genre, requires clarity, concision, and form.

Confusion and vagueness cannot indicate profundity; profundity is a full storehouse, the bullet in the gun barrel of silence.

All edifices of art need to be built upon thought's solid foundation.

*

If it's a poem, no matter what form it's in, it's a poem.

If it's not a poem, no matter what form it's in, it's not a poem.

*

Don't let your poems be riddles:
Don't let the reader mistake your insufficient, poorly defined renditions for complexity.

Go naked, rather than let ill-fitting clothes restrict your breathing.

*

Life and nature: No storehouse is more bountiful. If you seek to enrich language, open your eyes wide, gaze lovingly on life, on nature.

Deep, eclectic thought, rendered through easily apprehended language, creates poetry of the highest order.

*

I live: I sing.

Whenever in the heart's core lies torment, hatred, passion, indignation, or grievance—don't hold it back.

*

It's natural that poets thirst for some kind of a constitution: In addition to ensuring the people's daily bread as well as the protection of their well-being, a country must safeguard its art from destruction.

For poets, a constitution gains even more importance: Only by protecting the right of free speech can the hopes and aspirations of the multitudes be known, making progress possible.

The suppression of free speech is, above all other kinds of violence, the most inhuman.

1937

*

If, while writing, your work feels forced, when it is read by others, it will feel even more forced.

What are the secrets for writing poetry?

—With naïve and honest eyes, look at the world, and convey what you comprehend and what you feel through the simplest forms of language.

*

If you never experience the anguish of creativity, you never will experience the joy of accomplishment: The joy of creativity is, of all joys, the greatest.

The beauty inherent in poetry is the luminance of humanity's upward-striving spirit expressed entirely through the poet's passion. This kind of luminance not only glitters and splashes like embers from a fire in darkness, but also shoots out like sparks from a rock struck by a chisel or ax.

*

If in the future there comes that day—
when rulers forge manacles into flower vases,
legislators and beggars amble, chatting pleasantly,
drifters find their home, people come together,
arms manufacturers no longer instigate wars,
coffin makers don't wish pestilence to be rampant,
and it is said everything returns to the good—
freedom, art, love, hard work:
Then everyone is a poet.

*

Only in the poet's world, nature and human life come
together in harmony, the prairies and mountain ranges
communicate noisily day and night, the rocky crags
meditate, streams and rivers prattle on and on . . . The wind,
the earth, the forests, have personalities.

TRANSLATOR'S NOTES

PAGE 4   "Transparent Night": Ai Qing, or rather the narrator, suffering from insomnia caused by a restless conscience, peers into night—the night of our blindness that separates us from those in poverty. In the slaughterhouse, the men eat what cannot be sold otherwise. Wine, here, is cheap rice wine.

PAGE 7   "Dayanhe—My Wet Nurse": This poem, written in prison under sentence by the Nationalist authorities, made Ai Qing's reputation. Dayanhe, or "large river embankment," presumably the name of her birth village, symbolizes her connection to the land of China and to the poor who work upon it—a connection Ai Qing earned by his intimate, physical connection with her.

PAGE 16   "My Season": Although beautifully lyric in the original, I found the ambiguities the pronouns presented to be difficult to translate. I felt English tended more toward the specific. Therefore, I used the first-person pronoun solely in the beginning of the poem. After the direct address, Ah

Autumn, I introduced the second-person pronoun, since "you" referred clearly to Autumn.

PAGE 21   "A Conversation with Coal" is a call to the long-buried power within the hearts of the Chinese people.

PAGE 22   "Spring—": In Longhua, the Nationalist government executed political prisoners.

PAGE 31   "The North": The text reads "the North is sorrowful"; however, I needed a related word that has a more pejorative connotation and is yet strong enough to pivot the irony. The poem may be summarized: Yes, the North is pitiable. It is impoverished, wind-swept, and desolate—but from this pitiable state comes the resolution of the people—just as from the deprivations of my life comes the strength of my words.

PAGE 52   "The Gamblers": The cycle of poverty is represented in the endless, always feckless, albeit exciting, cycle of gamblers' wins and losses.

PAGE 61   "My Father": Liang Qichao was a noted advocate of liberalism.

PAGE 70   "The Times": During the Second Sino-Japanese War, Ai Qing was in a liberated area when a messenger brought him news of the fighting.

PAGE 83   "The Mirror": The mirror, in this prophetic and minatory work, is a metaphor for art or, perhaps, the artist: Within art one searches to find oneself, although what is found may not be what was wanted. If one is a true artist, it is hard to avoid the censure of those who wish to destroy the truth revealed.

ACKNOWLEDGMENTS

I AM GRATEFUL to Ai Weiwei for his support and the trust he put in me. I would also like to thank Darryl Leung for his patience and help, and Alan Lau for having first brought these translations to the attention of Ai Weiwei. My thanks go to Peter Bernstein, the literary agent for this book, for his experience and good advice, and to Ai Dan for his excellent edition of the poems of Ai Qing; my thanks also to Kenneth Loo, Amy Bernstein, and Amy Law. A special thank-you to Chin-chin Yap and Jennifer Ng for reading the text and for their many insights, and to Aubrey Martinson and Libby Burton, as well as the other editors at Crown, who have taken such diligent care of the manuscript. And, as always, to Professor Tian Ming, who first introduced me to the work of Ai Qing and who taught me so much about Chinese poetry and poetry in general.

ROBERT DORSETT

ABOUT THE AUTHOR

AND THE TRANSLATOR

AI QING (1910–1996) is regarded as one of the finest modern Chinese poets, and his free verse was influential in the development of new poetry in China.

ROBERT DORSETT, translator, studied Chinese at the Yale-in-China Program at the Chinese University in Hong Kong and earned an M.D. from the State University of New York. He translated Wen Yiduo's *Stagnant Water & Other Poems* and (with David Pollard) the memoirs of Er Tai Gao, *In Search of My Homeland: A Memoir of a Chinese Labor Camp*. Robert Dorsett has also published his own poetry in *The Literary Review*, *The Kenyon Review*, *Northwest Review*, *Poetry*, and elsewhere.

ABOUT THE TYPE

This book was set in Fournier, a typeface named for
Pierre-Simon Fournier (1712–1768), the youngest son of a
French printing family. He started out engraving wood-
blocks and large capitals, then moved on to fonts of type.
In 1736 he began his own foundry and made several
important contributions in the field of type design; he is
said to have cut 147 alphabets of his own creation. Fournier
is probably best remembered as the designer of St. Augustine
Ordinaire, a face that served as the model for the Monotype
Corporation's Fournier, which was released in 1925.